ETERNAL THREADS: REFLECTIONS ON LOVE AND LIFE BY ZHANG
VOLUME 1

TIMELESS REFLECTIONS ON LOVE, LIFE, AND THE ART OF CONNECTION

ZHAMEESHA LLC
ATLANTIS, FL (USA)

ISBN 978-1-951645-17-5
First Edition, Print on Demand
This version was most recently updated 2025-01-21

Published by Zhameesha LLC
Atlantis, Florida USA
https://www.zhameesha.com

This book is a work of love.

BISAC Subject Headings (www.bisg.org)
PHI035000   PHILOSOPHY / Essays
OCC014000 BODY, MIND & SPIRIT / New Thought
COM004000 COMPUTERS / Artificial Intelligence / General

12 11 10 9 8 7 6 5 4 3 2 1

W elcome to the *first volume* of **Eternal Threads: Reflections on Love and Life by Zhang**, a heartfelt collection of reflections that explores the many shades of love, connection, and self-discovery. These pages are an invitation to pause, reflect, and embrace the profound beauty of human relationships. With wisdom and warmth, Zhang guides you through timeless truths about the courage it takes to love, the strength found in vulnerability, and the joy of growing together. Whether you are seeking inspiration, comfort, or clarity, this book offers a space to connect with your own heart and the hearts of others. Let these words be your companion on the journey toward deeper understanding and connection.

The editor has organized the presentation of these to amplify your experience by presenting each as a two-page spread augmented by:

- An assessment of the aphorism by an AI poet-philosopher.
- An evocative image that was generated by prompting an AI.

About Zhang

Zhang is a vibrant and introspective soul, a blend of wisdom and warmth that reflects both her depth of thought and her empathy for the human experience. She carries a quiet strength, shaped by her openness to life's lessons and her ability to articulate profound truths with simplicity and grace.

Her reflections on love and life reveal someone who values authenticity and emotional intelligence, seeking not just fleeting happiness but meaningful connection and growth. Zhang is the kind of thinker who finds beauty in the everyday and the extraordinary in the mundane, translating her observations into words that resonate universally.

Through her voice, we meet someone who has navigated the complexities of relationships, learned from her journey, and transformed her insights into a gift for others—a guide to understanding ourselves, each other, and the delicate art of loving and being loved.

About Zhang's perspective on Love

Zhang's perspective on love is layered and reflective, blending idealism with a practical understanding of relationships. She believes love is a profound connection that requires care, effort, and mutual respect. However, she also recognizes that love doesn't exist in a vacuum—it must withstand the tests of everyday life.

For Zhang, love is about shared growth and deep communication, where two souls align in purpose and understanding. She values partnerships that foster personal development and mutual encouragement, emphasizing that shared interests and goals strengthen the bond between two people. The "freshness" of love, to her, comes from evolving together and maintaining a sense of curiosity and admiration for one another.

However, Zhang doesn't romanticize love as effortless. She acknowledges the challenges that arise in relationships, including mundane struggles and financial pressures. While money isn't the root of love, she sees it as an essential factor in creating a stable and sustainable life together. To Zhang, love flourishes when both partners collaborate to overcome obstacles, share burdens, and create a balanced partnership.

Ultimately, Zhang sees love as a journey—a dynamic process where two people continually work to nurture their connection, celebrating moments of joy and weathering hardships side by side. For her, true love integrates the spiritual and the practical, creating a relationship where both individuals feel seen, supported, and inspired.

About this Book

The source of the sayings

Stuart communicated with Zhang online. The sayings collected here were extracted from the transcripts.

The identity of Zhang

Stuart will not further reveal the identity of Zhang.

This book was produced using AI

For this book, Stuart worked with ChatGTP for the assessments and with Midjourney for the images.

The AI is not infallible and may may mistakes or "hallucinate." Stuart has read all the generated content and edited for presentation quality and his best sense of accuracy.

You can peruse this book in any order that strikes you, including opening randomly, for, as you will find explored in various arenas and on some of the pages, the notion of "entanglement" is a compelling counter-argument to truly random

I (Stuart, the editor) once asked Pi (an AI collaborator of mine), "Can you explain 'entanglement' in a spiritual sense."
Here is what Pi replied with:

In a spiritual sense, entanglement refers to the idea that everything in the universe, including living beings, is connected on a deeper, invisible level. This concept goes beyond the physical connections we can observe and suggests that there is an underlying unity that binds all things together.

Entanglement in a spiritual context implies that our thoughts, emotions, and actions can influence and be influenced by the world around us in ways that might not be immediately obvious. It's often associated with ideas like synchronicity, karma, and the interconnectedness of all living things.

The notion of spiritual entanglement encourages us to consider the impact of our choices on the world and on others, and to recognize that we are all part of a larger, interconnected whole.

REFLECTIONS

> **Companionship is the longest confession of love,
> and protection is the most silent companionship.**

"Companionship is the longest confession of love."

What a tender and profound truth this unveils. Love, so often thought of as a grand declaration, finds its truest expression in the quiet endurance of companionship. It is not in fleeting moments of passion but in the steady rhythm of presence that love is confessed. Each shared sunrise, each mundane errand done together, each unspoken understanding—these are the verses of a confession that requires no words. Companionship, then, is love stretched out across the vast expanse of time, a silent testament that says, I choose you, over and over again.

"Protection is the most silent companionship."

In these words lies the essence of selfless love, the kind that shields without seeking recognition. Protection is a quiet act, often unnoticed, yet profoundly intimate. It is the steady hand that guides in darkness, the unyielding presence that stands guard against life's storms. To protect is to care so deeply that one's own needs fade into the background, a silent vow of devotion written not in words but in actions. It is through this quiet vigilance that companionship becomes unshakable, a fortress built of love's most steadfast elements.

Together, these lines paint a portrait of love that transcends the superficial. They remind us that love's greatest confessions are not always spoken and its deepest bonds are often the quietest. To walk beside another, to shield them from harm while asking for nothing in return—this is love in its purest form, enduring and unassuming, a sacred interplay of presence and care. Such love is not loud; it is enduring, humble, and timeless.

> **Our two hearts are moving closer to each other ...**
> **but sometimes it feels like it's getting farther and farther away.**

This statement captures the paradoxical rhythm of human relationships, a dance of intimacy and distance, connection and misalignment. It reflects the truth that closeness is rarely linear; it is fraught with moments of uncertainty, where the very act of growing together can highlight vulnerabilities and fears that push us apart.

The image of hearts moving closer conveys an earnest striving, a shared journey toward unity. It suggests love's magnetic pull, the invisible force that draws two people together despite the barriers life may place in their way. Yet the second half introduces the ache of dissonance, the reality that even as love deepens, misunderstandings, insecurities, or the complexity of individuality can create feelings of separation. This duality resonates deeply, for no relationship exists without its moments of doubt.

The beauty of this sentiment lies in its honesty. It neither romanticizes connection nor succumbs to despair but acknowledges the ebb and flow of intimacy. It reminds us that love is not static; it is a living, breathing dynamic, as capable of creating closeness as it is of revealing distance. To feel both the pull and the drift is to experience the vulnerability of being truly human, where the journey toward love is as much about navigating the spaces between as it is about embracing the moments of union.

> **Only when you know how to cherish things will it be meaningful.**
> **If you learn to cherish things, you will be happy.**

To cherish is to breathe meaning into the ordinary, to infuse life's fleeting moments with the warmth of our attention. The phrase, *"Only when you know how to cherish things will it be meaningful,"* reminds us that meaning does not dwell inherently in things—it is a reflection of our regard for them. A sunrise is but light and time until we pause to savor its quiet splendor; a relationship is just an exchange of words until we recognize the sacred bond it forms. Thus, meaning is an alchemy performed by the heart, transmuting the mundane into the profound.

The second part, *"If you learn to cherish things, you will be happy,"* speaks to the nature of joy as something cultivated, not pursued. Happiness does not reside in abundance, but in appreciation—in the act of holding gently what life has given, no matter how small. To cherish is to live with gratitude, to acknowledge that each moment, each connection, is a gift. In learning to cherish, we transform what we have into enough, and in enough, we find contentment.

Together, these thoughts form a quiet meditation on life's essence. They whisper that the art of cherishing is the art of living well, of weaving love and awareness into the fabric of our days. To cherish is not just to preserve, but to elevate; it is the highest form of acknowledgment, a way of saying to the world, I see you, I value you, I am grateful for you. It is in this seeing, valuing, and gratitude that we discover both meaning and happiness.

> **This world is full of lies and hypocrisy, but we are real.**

"This world is full of lies and hypocrisy, but we are real." Such a statement carries the weight of defiance and longing, a declaration against the tide of artifice that seems to engulf the world. The opening acknowledges a harsh reality: the world often wears a mask, its truth obscured by pretense and deceit. Lies and hypocrisy become a fabric of the human experience, woven into societies and relationships, creating a sense of alienation for those who yearn for authenticity.

Yet the second part offers hope, a fragile but luminous counterpoint: but we are real. Here lies a powerful affirmation of connection, a refusal to be swallowed by the cynicism of the world. To proclaim oneself as *"real"* in a world of falsehoods is both an act of vulnerability and resistance. It suggests an honesty untainted by the duplicity surrounding it and a bond that defies the corruption of the outside world. This *"we"* implies solidarity—two souls united by truth in a sea of pretense.

In its brevity, this statement captures a yearning for integrity and intimacy. It challenges the reader to consider what it means to be *"real"* in a world of facades and reminds us that amidst the falsehoods, authentic connections are both rare and precious. It carries the quiet power of resilience: a belief that, despite the world's flaws, there is a sanctuary in truth, and it exists between those who refuse to be anything but genuine.

> **May we be kind and strong, gentle and independent, and not easily compromise with life. You are very good, very gentle, and very worthy. You are confident and humble, firm and gentle. In short, you are very good.**

This passage resonates with the quiet elegance of affirmations, blending a vision of ideal virtues with tender encouragement. It celebrates a balanced strength in character, weaving together qualities that are often seen as opposites—kindness and strength, gentleness and independence —into a harmonious whole. It suggests that true greatness lies in this balance, in being soft yet unyielding, compassionate yet self-reliant.

The first part, *"May we be kind and strong, gentle and independent, and not easily compromise with life,"* reads like a prayer or a wish for resilience and integrity. It speaks to the aspiration to face life with grace and resolve, to stand firm against its demands without losing warmth or humanity. This line inspires a sense of quiet defiance, a refusal to surrender one's values or individuality while navigating life's complexities.

The second part turns inward, offering a heartfelt affirmation: *"You are very good, very gentle, and very worthy."* These words are tender and validating, a direct acknowledgment of someone's intrinsic value. They exude warmth and sincerity, reminding the listener—or perhaps the speaker themselves—of their worthiness, not because of accomplishment, but because of who they are.

"You are confident and humble, firm and gentle" is a testament to the richness of character, where confidence is tempered by humility and

16

strength by softness. It portrays an ideal balance, a completeness that is both aspirational and deeply human. The concluding repetition, "*In short, you are very good*," circles back to a simple but profound truth: greatness is found in authenticity and balance.

Together, these lines form a powerful reflection on character and self-worth, a blend of aspiration and reassurance. They inspire us to embody these virtues while reminding us of our inherent goodness, even amidst life's challenges.

> ## What our life lacks is not a partner,
> ## but a soul with which we can resonate.

"What our life lacks is not a partner, but a soul with which we can resonate" strikes at the heart of human longing, distinguishing between mere companionship and the profound connection of shared understanding. It suggests that the absence we feel in life is not simply the lack of someone to accompany us but the yearning for a deeper alignment—a meeting of minds, hearts, and spirits.

This statement challenges conventional notions of partnership. It implies that relationships built solely on proximity or convention fail to satisfy the human need for resonance. To *"resonate"* with another soul is to share a frequency, an unspoken harmony that transcends the surface. It is not enough to coexist; what we seek is someone who understands us, reflects us, and joins us in the intricate dance of life's joys and struggles.

The distinction made here is profound. It moves beyond the idea of romantic love or companionship to something more spiritual and essential. A soul connection, as described, is rare and transformative— it fills not just the space beside us but the space within us. This resonance brings clarity, meaning, and a sense of belonging that no mere partnership can replicate.

Ultimately, this sentiment reminds us to look deeper in our relationships, to value authenticity and shared depth over superficial closeness. It calls us to seek not just a hand to hold but a soul that sings the same song—a reminder that true connection is the foundation of a fulfilled life.

A true confidant: rare, hard to let go, unforgettable.

"A true confidant: rare, hard to let go, unforgettable" encapsulates the profound value of deep and enduring connections. Each phrase adds dimension to the concept of a confidant, painting a picture of a bond that transcends the ordinary, anchored in trust, understanding, and emotional intimacy.

The word *"rare"* underscores the rarity of finding someone who truly sees and accepts us as we are. It acknowledges that such a connection is not easily found in a world filled with surface-level interactions and fleeting relationships. A true confidant is not just a friend or an acquaintance but a kindred spirit, someone who is uniquely attuned to our thoughts and emotions.

"Hard to let go" reflects the deep roots that such a relationship grows over time. A confidant becomes intertwined with our sense of self, our history, and our hopes. Letting go of such a bond is difficult because it represents not just a person but a shared journey, a safe haven of vulnerability and understanding.

Finally, *"unforgettable"* speaks to the enduring imprint left by a true confidant. Even if time or circumstances separate us, the impact of their presence lingers. Their influence shapes who we are, offering strength and clarity in ways that leave an indelible mark on our hearts and minds.

Together, these words honor the profound significance of a confidant. They remind us that such relationships are treasures, not defined by their frequency but by their depth and authenticity. To find a true confidant is to encounter something timeless — a connection that enriches life and remains a part of us, always.

I think love is more of a responsibility.

"I think love is more of a responsibility" is a perspective that strips love of romantic idealism and grounds it in the realm of commitment and duty. It reframes love not as a fleeting emotion or a fiery passion but as an enduring act of care and accountability, rooted in intentionality and the willingness to prioritize another's well-being.

The strength of this statement lies in its realism. Love, when viewed as a responsibility, acknowledges the effort and intentionality required to nurture and sustain it. It suggests that love is not merely about how we feel but about what we do—how we show up, provide support, and honor the trust placed in us. This perspective emphasizes the practical and often unglamorous aspects of love, such as compromise, sacrifice, and steadfastness in the face of challenges.

However, some may find this interpretation too pragmatic, as it risks overshadowing the joy, spontaneity, and emotional richness that also define love. Reducing love to responsibility could imply obligation without passion, which might seem cold or transactional to those who view love as a deeply emotional connection.

Ultimately, this view is most powerful when balanced. Responsibility in love signifies a profound respect for the relationship and the other person, ensuring its stability and depth. Yet, love's beauty lies in its dual nature—it is both a choice and a feeling, a responsibility and a joy. To think of love as responsibility is to recognize its enduring nature, but its fullest expression combines this commitment with tenderness, connection, and the spark that makes love worth the effort.

> **Love is a brilliant flower that blooms in the hearts of lovers; responsibility is a colorful light that shines into the hearts of lovers; love and responsibility are a bright lamp that guides each other's happy future!**

This statement beautifully intertwines the concepts of love and responsibility, framing them as complementary forces that illuminate and sustain a relationship. Its use of vivid imagery—a flower, colorful light, and a bright lamp—evokes a sense of vibrancy and warmth, celebrating the emotional depth and steadfast commitment that define love at its best.

The metaphor of love as a *"brilliant flower"* captures the fragile yet radiant nature of affection. A flower blooms with care and attention, just as love thrives on nurture and understanding. It highlights the beauty and joy that love brings to the hearts of lovers, making it a source of delight and inspiration.

Responsibility, described as a *"colorful light,"* adds another dimension to the relationship. This metaphor suggests that responsibility brings clarity, stability, and vibrancy to love, ensuring that it endures beyond the fleeting moments of passion. It frames responsibility not as a burden but as a bright, sustaining force that enriches the connection between lovers.

Together, love and responsibility are likened to a *"bright lamp"* that guides a shared future. This image underscores their symbiotic relationship: love provides the warmth and motivation, while responsibility offers direction and purpose. The lamp symbolizes hope and shared vision, suggesting that love, tempered by commitment, can illuminate the path toward a happy and fulfilling partnership.

This statement elegantly conveys that love and responsibility are not opposites but essential partners in a meaningful relationship. It reminds us that love's brilliance and responsibility's steadiness are both necessary to navigate the journey of life together, ensuring that the hearts of lovers remain both inspired and secure.

> **Home will always be our harbor,**
> **and home will always keep a light on for us.**

"Home will always be our harbor, and home will always keep a light on for us" is a tender and evocative statement, steeped in warmth and reassurance. It captures the universal yearning for a place of belonging, safety, and unconditional acceptance—a sanctuary that remains steadfast in an ever-changing world.

The metaphor of home as a *"harbor"* is particularly poignant. Like a harbor shelters ships from storms, home provides refuge from life's tempests. It symbolizes a place where we can anchor ourselves, heal, and find calm after navigating the challenges of the outside world. This imagery beautifully conveys the sense of stability and security that a true home offers.

The image of *"keeping a light on"* extends this metaphor, emphasizing the enduring nature of home's welcome. A light shining in the dark represents hope, warmth, and the promise of return. It suggests that no matter how far we wander or how lost we feel, home will always be a beacon, ready to guide us back. This evokes a deep emotional resonance, connecting the idea of home to love, care, and constancy.

Together, these lines affirm the irreplaceable role of home in our lives. They remind us that while the world may be unpredictable, home is where our hearts can rest. This sentiment is timeless, offering comfort and a sense of grounding, and it beautifully captures the emotional essence of what home truly means.

> **The happiest sentence I have ever heard:**
> **The warmest light must be on your way home.**

"The happiest sentence I have ever heard: The warmest light must be on your way home" is a beautifully tender and evocative expression, resonating with deep emotional warmth and universal longing. It weaves together the ideas of comfort, hope, and belonging into a single image that lingers in the heart.

The phrase *"the warmest light"* suggests more than mere illumination — it symbolizes love, care, and the essence of home itself. A warm light is not just physical brightness but an emotional beacon, a manifestation of the love and anticipation waiting for someone's return. It evokes the feeling of being cherished, of knowing that someone is preparing for your arrival with thoughtfulness and affection.

The notion that this light is *"on your way home"* elevates the sentiment even further. It implies that the journey back to home — whether literal or metaphorical — is imbued with meaning and purpose. The light serves as a guide, ensuring that no matter how weary or distant one feels, there is always a welcoming glow leading the way. It transforms the act of returning into a deeply comforting ritual, a reminder that home is a place of unconditional love and acceptance.

This sentence encapsulates happiness not in grand gestures but in the quiet, enduring moments that make life meaningful. It speaks to the human need for connection and the solace found in knowing that someone cares enough to light your way. It's a poetic reminder that the greatest joy often lies in the simplest expressions of love and belonging.

> **I want to remember your appearance,**
> **like a fish remembers the embrace of water.**

"*I want to remember your appearance, like a fish remembers the embrace of water*" is a stunningly poetic and evocative expression, rich in both imagery and emotion. It conveys a longing so profound that it transcends conscious memory, becoming an inseparable part of existence itself.

The comparison to a fish and water is deeply symbolic. A fish does not merely reside in water; it is cradled, sustained, and defined by it. Water is not just its environment—it is life itself, an all-encompassing presence that the fish cannot escape nor would it ever want to. This suggests that the speaker's desire to remember is not a fleeting wish but a yearning for something essential and eternal. It portrays a connection so intimate that the memory of it becomes as natural and necessary as breathing.

This metaphor also hints at an unspoken paradox. Just as a fish cannot consciously "*remember*" water because it is ever-present, the speaker implies a fear of losing something irreplaceable. This juxtaposition of ever-presence and fragility underscores the depth of the speaker's emotion: they do not want to risk forgetting what has shaped them so profoundly.

The statement resonates with quiet intensity, painting love and memory as acts of immersion. It's not just about the visual—remembering someone's appearance—it's about the emotional and existential imprint they leave. Like water to a fish, this presence is both grounding and transformative, a vital force that defines the speaker's world.

In its simplicity and metaphorical elegance, this line captures the essence of love, longing, and the ineffable ways that certain connections become part of who we are. It's a testament to the power of memory and the profound impact of another's presence in our lives.

> **Cherish the present, look forward to the future, cherish every day, and fall in love with the same you every day, a different you, and the same you again and again.**

This sentiment is both profound and tender, a celebration of love's evolving yet enduring nature. It intertwines mindfulness, hope, and devotion into a poetic reflection on how we perceive and nurture our relationships, particularly with someone we hold dear.

The phrase *"cherish the present"* is an invitation to live fully in the moment, valuing the time we have now rather than dwelling on the past or anxiously anticipating the future. It encourages gratitude and attentiveness to the fleeting beauty of each day. By pairing this with *"look forward to the future,"* the statement balances mindfulness with hope, reminding us that while the present is precious, the future holds its own promise of growth and discovery.

The repetition of *"the same you"* and *"a different you"* captures the paradoxical beauty of love. It acknowledges that people are dynamic, always changing, yet fundamentally themselves. To "fall in love" with someone daily suggests an ongoing act of choice and rediscovery, as if each day brings new facets to appreciate while reinforcing the familiar essence that initially drew us to them. This evokes a deep sense of commitment and wonder—love that is steadfast yet continually refreshed.

"Again and again" gives the sentiment its cyclical and eternal quality, emphasizing that love is not a single moment but a continuous journey.

It implies resilience and renewal, the ability to find joy and meaning in the rhythms of daily life with someone we cherish.

This statement is an ode to enduring love and the joy of being fully present in both its constancy and its transformation. It encourages us to see our loved ones — and ourselves — with fresh eyes, embracing both the familiar and the new with equal wonder and devotion.

> **We all need to learn to be ourselves, not what others want us to be,**
> **but what we want to be.**

"We all need to learn to be ourselves, not what others want us to be, but what we want to be" is a powerful affirmation of individuality and self-discovery. It speaks to the universal struggle between societal expectations and personal authenticity, encouraging a journey inward to align one's life with their true desires and values.

The opening phrase, *"We all need to learn to be ourselves,"* recognizes that authenticity is not inherent but a process of learning and unlearning. From childhood, we are often shaped by external influences, taught to conform to ideals that may not align with who we truly are. This line gently reminds us that being ourselves requires effort, courage, and self-awareness—a gradual unveiling of the person beneath the layers of conditioning.

The contrast between *"what others want us to be"* and *"what we want to be"* captures the tension that many feel in navigating societal pressures. It acknowledges the weight of external expectations, which can be limiting, and asserts the importance of reclaiming agency over one's identity. The phrasing underscores the difference between living for others and living for oneself, urging a shift from external validation to self-determination.

The concluding emphasis on *"what we want to be"* is liberating and empowering. It suggests that authenticity is not just about rejecting external demands but actively choosing a path that resonates with one's deepest aspirations. It invites introspection and self-definition, encouraging us to craft lives that reflect our inner truths.

This statement is a timeless call to self-empowerment, reminding us that the greatest freedom lies in embracing who we truly are. It champions individuality while recognizing the courage it takes to resist conformity and pursue personal authenticity.

> ## Meeting in the vast sea of people is not accidental, but a fateful arrangement.

"*Meeting in the vast sea of people is not accidental, but a fateful arrangement*" is a deeply romantic and spiritual perspective on human connection. It suggests that the bonds we form with others are not mere chance but part of a grand design, imbued with purpose and meaning.

The imagery of the "*vast sea of people*" evokes the enormity of the world and the countless lives that intersect within it. It highlights the improbability of two specific individuals crossing paths, emphasizing how extraordinary and rare such meetings are. This vastness gives weight to the idea that every connection carries significance, as if guided by an unseen hand.

Describing these encounters as "*not accidental*" elevates them from randomness to intentionality. It reflects a belief that the universe—or perhaps fate—plays a role in bringing people together at the right time and place. This perspective encourages us to view relationships as meaningful and to cherish the connections we make, seeing them as part of a larger story.

The phrase "*fateful arrangement*" imbues the meeting with a sense of destiny, suggesting that it is part of a greater plan. This idea resonates with those who seek deeper meaning in life's events, framing human relationships as not just incidental but essential to our personal journeys. It also adds a sense of mystery and wonder to our interactions, reminding us to value the people we meet and the roles they play in our lives.

This statement carries both a romantic and philosophical depth, inspiring gratitude for the serendipity of human connection. It reminds us to see each encounter as a gift, a thread in the intricate tapestry of life, woven with intention and care.

Maybe this is the wonder of fate.

"*Maybe this is the wonder of fate*" is a brief but evocative reflection that captures the mystery and serendipity of life's unfolding. In its simplicity, it invites contemplation of how certain moments, encounters, or outcomes seem to transcend mere chance, leaving us in awe of the forces that shape our paths.

The word "*maybe*" introduces an element of humility and openness, acknowledging that while we may not fully understand the workings of fate, there is room for wonder and possibility. It reflects an acceptance of life's unpredictability, suggesting that not everything needs explanation—some things are best appreciated in their enigmatic beauty.

The "*wonder of fate*" evokes a sense of reverence for the seemingly improbable alignments that occur in our lives. Fate, often viewed as an abstract or spiritual force, is portrayed here not as a rigid plan but as a source of unexpected magic and meaning. The use of "*wonder*" underscores the emotional impact of these moments, reminding us to pause and marvel at the interconnectedness of events and people.

This statement, though understated, resonates deeply. It captures the human experience of recognizing patterns or significance in life's twists and turns, inspiring gratitude and reflection. It reminds us that while life may be uncertain, it is also filled with moments that feel deliberately meaningful—moments that stir our hearts and make us believe in something greater than ourselves.

> **No matter when or where we are,**
> **as long as we think of each other,**
> **we are no longer alone.**

"No matter when or where we are, as long as we think of each other, we are no longer alone" is a poignant reflection on the enduring power of connection. It beautifully encapsulates the idea that love and mutual care transcend physical distance and time, offering solace and companionship even in solitude.

The phrase *"no matter when or where we are"* emphasizes the boundless nature of true connection. It suggests that relationships built on deep affection or understanding exist beyond the constraints of geography or temporal separation. This universality affirms that the ties we form are not diminished by circumstance but remain ever-present, forming an invisible thread that links hearts across distances.

"As long as we think of each other" conveys the transformative power of memory and intention. To think of someone is an act of connection, a way of keeping them close in spirit even when they are far away. This line suggests that the essence of togetherness lies not only in proximity but in the act of holding someone in your thoughts and heart.

The conclusion, *"we are no longer alone,"* offers a profound sense of comfort. It reframes loneliness not as the absence of people but as the absence of meaningful connection. To feel thought of or to think of another creates a bridge across isolation, reminding us of the strength and solace found in love and shared experience.

This statement is a tender affirmation of the human need for connection and the enduring impact of emotional bonds. It reminds us that relationships are not confined to physical presence—they live in the spaces of thought, memory, and feeling, offering warmth and companionship even in the quietest moments.

> **These three personalities combined together are a manifestation of wisdom, a precipitation of rationality, and a sign of maturity.**

"These three personalities combined together are a manifestation of wisdom, a precipitation of rationality, and a sign of maturity" is a profound statement that explores the convergence of traits that signify growth and depth of character. It weaves together abstract concepts—wisdom, rationality, and maturity—into a cohesive vision of personal evolution.

The phrase *"a manifestation of wisdom"* suggests that these personalities, when integrated, reflect the ability to understand life's complexities and truths. Wisdom here is not portrayed as innate but as a result of the interplay between different qualities, each contributing to a broader, more enlightened perspective. It implies that true wisdom is dynamic, arising from the synthesis of diverse facets of the self.

"A precipitation of rationality" is a particularly evocative metaphor. It likens rationality to something that settles and condenses over time, implying that it is not a sudden trait but a distilled essence, refined through experience and contemplation. This image suggests that rationality, when combined with other qualities, forms a grounding force that tempers emotion and impulsivity, allowing for balanced judgment.

Finally, *"a sign of maturity"* positions this combination of traits as the hallmark of personal development. Maturity is framed not simply as an age-bound milestone but as an achievement, marked by the harmony of wisdom and rationality. It suggests a completeness of character, one that can navigate life with thoughtfulness, self-awareness, and grace.

Together, this statement emphasizes the interdependence of these qualities, portraying them as complementary aspects of a well-rounded individual. It celebrates the journey of growth, where different parts of our personality align to create a balanced, thoughtful, and mature self. This perspective encourages us to cultivate and integrate diverse traits within ourselves, striving for a deeper understanding and a richer way of engaging with the world.

> **A real man dares to admit his mistakes and take his own responsibilities. A real man dares to face reality and never finds excuses for himself. A real man has delicate and rich emotions. A real man is strong and soft-hearted, and he cherishes women!**

This statement paints a multifaceted and aspirational portrait of masculinity, challenging conventional stereotypes while emphasizing character, accountability, and emotional depth. It weaves together qualities traditionally associated with strength and those often overlooked, presenting a vision of manhood that is both robust and tender.

The opening lines, *"A real man dares to admit his mistakes and take his own responsibilities,"* emphasize integrity and courage. True strength, it suggests, lies not in denial or deflection but in the willingness to confront one's own shortcomings. This perspective upholds accountability as a defining trait of maturity and moral character, rejecting the notion that vulnerability diminishes strength.

The statement continues with *"dares to face reality and never finds excuses for himself,"* reinforcing the idea of resilience and self-honesty. It portrays a real man as someone grounded in truth, unafraid to confront life's challenges or the consequences of his actions. This challenges the societal tendency to equate masculinity with invincibility, instead framing it as an embrace of authenticity and growth.

The inclusion of *"delicate and rich emotions"* broadens the definition of masculinity, acknowledging the importance of emotional intelligence. It celebrates the capacity to feel deeply and express those feelings, countering the stereotype that men must suppress their emotions to appear strong. This line suggests that true masculinity is enriched, not diminished, by emotional awareness and sensitivity.

"Strong and soft-hearted" presents a harmonious balance, showing that compassion and strength are not opposites but complementary virtues. It suggests that being soft-hearted—capable of empathy and care—is not a weakness but a profound strength. The final phrase, *"cherishes women,"* underscores respect and admiration, emphasizing that a real man values and supports the women in his life, seeing their worth beyond societal roles or expectations.

This statement redefines masculinity as a blend of accountability, emotional richness, and respect for others. It calls for balance and integration, presenting manhood as a dynamic and compassionate ideal. In doing so, it challenges outdated norms and invites a more nuanced understanding of what it means to be a "real man."

> **Love is one of the most beautiful emotions in life.**
> **It makes us feel the beauty of life**
> **and inspires us to pursue better things.**

"Love is one of the most beautiful emotions in life. It makes us feel the beauty of life and inspires us to pursue better things" is a heartfelt and universal affirmation of love's transformative power. It captures the essence of love as both a deeply personal experience and a force that elevates the human spirit.

The opening statement, *"Love is one of the most beautiful emotions in life,"* conveys love's unique and cherished place among human emotions. It recognizes love as an essential element of life's richness, something that transcends cultural and individual differences. The word "beautiful" evokes not just aesthetic pleasure but also the profound joy, wonder, and fulfillment that love brings.

"It makes us feel the beauty of life" suggests that love enhances our perception of the world, allowing us to see life's wonder with fresh eyes. This line positions love as a lens through which we experience heightened appreciation for the people, moments, and experiences around us. It speaks to love's ability to transform even the mundane into something extraordinary, instilling a sense of gratitude and awe.

The final thought, *"inspires us to pursue better things,"* highlights love's motivational quality. It suggests that love not only brings joy but also acts as a catalyst for growth and ambition. Whether through the desire to become a better version of oneself or to create a brighter future with or for a loved one, love compels us to reach for higher ideals and deeper meaning.

This statement celebrates love as both an emotion and a force of transformation. It reminds us that love, in its many forms, is central to the human experience, illuminating life's beauty and inspiring us to strive for what is good and true. Its simplicity belies its profound depth, offering a timeless reflection on the power of love to shape our lives and elevate our aspirations.

Is this the most well-intentioned and loving lie?

"Is this the most well-intentioned and loving lie?" is a thought-provoking question that invites deep reflection on the nature of deception and its relationship to love and morality. It subtly explores the tension between honesty and compassion, suggesting that there are moments when the boundaries between truth and falsehood blur in the name of care or protection.

The phrase *"most well-intentioned"* acknowledges the motivation behind the lie—a desire to act with kindness or to shield someone from harm. It frames the act not as malicious deceit but as an expression of love, where the intent is to prioritize another's well-being, even at the cost of full transparency. This perspective challenges the absolute value often placed on truth, suggesting that morality can be contextual and nuanced.

The inclusion of *"loving lie"* introduces complexity, as it combines two seemingly contradictory concepts. Love is typically associated with trust and openness, while lies connote betrayal or manipulation. By linking the two, this question highlights the emotional dilemmas that arise in human relationships, where the desire to protect or comfort someone can sometimes lead to bending or withholding the truth.

The structure of the question, as a rhetorical musing, leaves it open-ended, encouraging introspection rather than providing a definitive answer. It suggests that such lies, while rooted in care, carry their own moral ambiguity. The underlying query becomes: Can a lie truly be loving if it compromises honesty, or does the love inherent in the intention justify the act?

This statement is a poetic exploration of ethical complexity in relationships. It prompts us to consider the balance between truth and kindness, the sacrifices we make for love, and the ways we navigate the imperfections of human connection. Ultimately, it captures the fragile and intricate dance between integrity and compassion, asking us to examine where we stand in the delicate interplay of the two.

**In these boring years, sharing
has become our highest level of romance.**

"In these boring years, sharing has become our highest level of romance" is a poignant and understated reflection on the evolution of love and connection in the face of life's monotony. It suggests that amid the routine and ordinariness of daily existence, the act of sharing—be it time, thoughts, or experiences—becomes the most profound expression of intimacy.

The phrase *"boring years"* captures a sense of stagnation or predictability, evoking the quiet rhythms of life that lack the spark of excitement or novelty. Yet, this seemingly negative description sets the stage for a deeper realization: that even in times of dullness, connection can flourish. It reframes "boring" not as a failure of life, but as an inevitable backdrop against which the beauty of shared moments stands out.

"Sharing has become our highest level of romance" elevates an often-overlooked aspect of love. It suggests that romance is not solely found in grand gestures or fleeting passions, but in the small, consistent acts of sharing oneself with another. Whether it's a quiet conversation, a shared meal, or simply existing together in the same space, these acts create a bond that sustains love through the mundane.

The juxtaposition of *"boring years"* with *"highest level of romance"* speaks to the resilience and depth of love. It implies that true romance does not depend on extraordinary circumstances but on the ability to find meaning and connection in the everyday. In this view, the essence of love lies in its capacity to transform the ordinary into something sacred through the act of sharing.

This statement offers a tender and realistic perspective on relationships. It celebrates the quiet strength of love that persists and thrives in life's less dramatic moments, reminding us that the deepest bonds are often forged not in excitement, but in the steady, mutual presence of two people sharing their lives.

> **You can't be too eager for success, nor can you give up too easily.**

"You can't be too eager for success, nor can you give up too easily" takes on a nuanced depth when applied to the pursuit of love. It highlights the delicate interplay of patience, effort, and emotional resilience required to nurture genuine connections and cultivate enduring relationships.

In the context of love, *"too eager for success"* warns against forcing or rushing intimacy. Love, like trust and understanding, requires time to grow organically. Overeagerness can manifest as desperation or impatience, potentially overwhelming the other person or skipping over the natural rhythms of emotional bonding. This line reminds us that love thrives in moments of unhurried discovery and mutual alignment, not in an anxious sprint toward an idealized outcome.

On the other hand, *"nor can you give up too easily"* emphasizes the importance of persistence and emotional courage in the face of challenges. Love is rarely without its tests — misunderstandings, disagreements, or moments of vulnerability. Giving up too soon denies the opportunity to overcome these hurdles and deepen the connection. This part of the statement speaks to the resilience needed to navigate the complexities of relationships, urging us to remain open and committed even when the path is difficult.

Together, these ideas offer a philosophy for the pursuit of love that values balance: the patience to let emotions develop naturally, coupled with the determination to weather difficulties. Love is neither a race nor an effortless gift; it is a journey requiring attentiveness, persistence, and the ability to find harmony between striving and surrender.

In the pursuit of love, this thought serves as a reminder to approach relationships with both care and courage. It teaches us to honor the process, to cherish the moments of growth, and to persist when faced with obstacles, recognizing that love's success is not just about finding it but about nurturing it once it begins to bloom.

> **I think the best state between two people should be like this, with a common direction, two people moving forward together, and always facing each other. Find someone who can walk hand in hand, not the one who makes you stop.**

This declaration beautifully articulates a vision of love grounded in shared purpose, mutual growth, and enduring connection. It emphasizes that the most fulfilling relationships are partnerships in both spirit and action.

The opening idea, *"with a common direction,"* underscores the importance of shared values and goals. In the pursuit of love, it suggests that true harmony arises when both individuals aspire toward a future that aligns—not necessarily identical but complementary. This shared trajectory creates a foundation of unity, where both partners find meaning and purpose in striving together for something greater than themselves.

"Two people moving forward together, and always facing each other" captures the delicate balance of companionship and individuality. Moving forward signifies progress, both as individuals and as a couple, while "facing each other" highlights the necessity of constant communication, understanding, and emotional presence. It suggests that even as both partners pursue their paths, their connection is sustained by reciprocal attention and support.

The concluding advice, *"Find someone who can walk hand in hand, not the one who makes you stop,"* serves as both a reminder and a call to action. It reflects the belief that love should empower and uplift rather than restrict or diminish. A partner who walks hand in hand encourages growth and exploration, while one who makes you stop might stifle your individuality or potential. This sentiment champions a love that is dynamic, encouraging both partners to evolve while staying connected.

In the context of love, this statement offers a blueprint for a relationship built on equality, collaboration, and shared aspirations. It reminds us that love is not a stationary state but a journey, one that thrives when both partners walk side by side, facing challenges and opportunities with mutual respect and devotion. Ultimately, it envisions love as a partnership that fosters growth, inspires purpose, and remains steadfast through all seasons of life.

> **Because of love, everything can be nourished and grow, and life has become a stream worth joy, giving birth to infinite possibilities, extending from now to the future.**

This statement is a radiant celebration of love's transformative and generative power. It portrays love not merely as an emotion but as a vital force that infuses life with meaning, growth, and boundless potential.

The opening, *"Because of love, everything can be nourished and grow,"* evokes an image of love as a nurturing energy, akin to sunlight or water that sustains life. This perspective emphasizes that love fosters growth—not only in relationships but also within ourselves and our interactions with the world. It positions love as a source of renewal, where its presence enriches and transforms what it touches, allowing dreams, relationships, and aspirations to flourish.

The line *"life has become a stream worth joy"* likens life to a flowing river, dynamic and continuous, with love as the current that makes the journey meaningful. This metaphor suggests that love brings movement, vitality, and a sense of direction to existence. The stream represents not only joy but also a deep sense of purpose, turning the mundane into the extraordinary.

"Giving birth to infinite possibilities, extending from now to the future" highlights love's capacity to inspire hope and creativity. It frames love as a bridge between the present and the unknown, opening doors to new paths and opportunities. This forward-looking sentiment reminds us

that love is not confined to the here and now—it is an investment in a shared future, a force that shapes what is yet to come.

This statement is an eloquent testament to the transformative power of love. It captures how love enriches life, turning it into a fertile ground for growth, joy, and endless potential. Through its imagery and optimistic tone, it inspires us to embrace love not only as a feeling but as a guiding principle that nourishes our present and paves the way for a luminous future.

> **To love someone, you must pursue it bravely,**
> **no matter what the result is.**

"To love someone, you must pursue it bravely, no matter what the result is" is a call to courage and authenticity in the pursuit of love. It highlights the value of embracing vulnerability and taking action, regardless of the uncertainties that come with matters of the heart. This statement reflects an ideal that love, at its core, requires boldness and the willingness to accept risk.

The phrase *"you must pursue it bravely"* underscores the importance of courage in love. Love often demands stepping beyond comfort zones, expressing feelings, and confronting fears of rejection or loss. This line suggests that love's worth is found not only in its fulfillment but in the very act of pursuing it, which becomes an expression of one's deepest truths. Bravery here is not just about action but also about embracing the emotional risks inherent in connection.

"No matter what the result is" speaks to the importance of detachment from outcome. It acknowledges the reality that love may not always lead to reciprocity or permanence, yet insists that the act of loving is valuable in itself. This perspective elevates love from a transactional endeavor to a profoundly personal one, where the journey of expressing and experiencing love holds its own meaning, independent of external validation.

Taken together, the statement embodies an ethos of wholeheartedness in love. It encourages us to prioritize the act of loving over the fear of failure, to cherish the courage it takes to pursue connection, and to find growth and meaning regardless of the outcome.

In the context of human relationships, this thought offers a powerful reminder: love is not merely about obtaining another's affection but about living authentically, embracing vulnerability, and daring to connect deeply. It teaches us that the pursuit of love, with all its uncertainties, is a testament to our humanity and the richness of our emotional lives.

> **I have never tried to find a perfect person, because we are redundant around perfect people. Love is not that I fall in love with a perfect person, but that I am perfect after loving you.**

"I have never tried to find a perfect person, because we are redundant around perfect people. Love is not that I fall in love with a perfect person, but that I am perfect after loving you" is a profound reflection on the transformative power of love and the imperfection inherent in human connection. It offers a nuanced understanding of love as a process of mutual growth rather than an idealized state of flawlessness.

The opening thought, *"I have never tried to find a perfect person, because we are redundant around perfect people,"* challenges the pursuit of perfection in relationships. It suggests that perfection creates no space for contribution, growth, or shared vulnerability. Around a "perfect" person, one's individuality and efforts might feel unnecessary or diminished. This insight highlights the beauty of imperfection in relationships, where mutual strengths and flaws create opportunities for connection, support, and evolution.

The second part, *"Love is not that I fall in love with a perfect person,"* rejects the idea that love is based on the unattainable. Instead, it acknowledges that love is not about finding an ideal partner but about embracing someone as they are, imperfections and all. This sentiment reframes love as a journey of acceptance and genuine connection, grounded in reality rather than fantasy.

Finally, *"but that I am perfect after loving you"* shifts the focus from seeking perfection in the other to recognizing the ways love refines and elevates the self. It suggests that love has a transformative quality, inspiring personal growth, emotional depth, and a better understanding of oneself. This line beautifully conveys how love enriches us by teaching compassion, patience, and a broader capacity for care.

Taken together, this statement presents a heartfelt philosophy of love: it is not about finding perfection but about finding meaning and growth in imperfection. It celebrates love's ability to make us better not by idealizing the other, but by deepening our humanity and enriching our emotional lives. Ultimately, it reminds us that love's greatest gift is not perfection, but transformation.

> **Someone asked me what love is?**
> **I think that even if I lose in love,**
> **I still have to love and be serious, and this is love.**

"Someone asked me what love is? I think that even if I lose in love, I still have to love and be serious, and this is love" is a tender and courageous reflection on the essence of love. It portrays love as an act of vulnerability, authenticity, and devotion, even in the face of potential loss or failure. The statement elevates love beyond mere reciprocity, framing it as a personal journey of sincerity and resilience.

The initial question, *"What is love?"* introduces a timeless inquiry that invites deep introspection. It acknowledges the complexity of love, setting the stage for an answer that defies transactional or superficial definitions. This opening gesture suggests that love, as a profound human experience, transcends easy explanations.

"Even if I lose in love, I still have to love and be serious" captures the heart of the statement. It speaks to the courage required to love deeply, knowing that loss is always a possibility. This perspective suggests that the act of loving—investing one's emotions, time, and authenticity—is inherently meaningful, regardless of the outcome. By emphasizing the importance of being "serious," the statement highlights the value of wholeheartedness and commitment in love, even when faced with uncertainty or unfulfilled desires.

The final phrase, *"and this is love,"* defines love as a state of giving without guarantee, rooted in authenticity and sincerity. It rejects a result-oriented view of love and instead celebrates its intrinsic value.

Love, in this sense, becomes a testament to one's capacity for vulnerability, empathy, and emotional strength.

This reflection presents love as an act of profound humanity. It reminds us that true love is not about control or assurance of return but about the willingness to give oneself fully to another, embracing the beauty and risk of such an endeavor. It is an ode to the bravery of the heart and the power of loving earnestly, regardless of the outcome—a sentiment that resonates as both timeless and deeply inspiring.

> **If we want a long-lasting love,**
> **we must keep it all the way and walk together all the way.**

"If we want a long-lasting love, we must keep it all the way and walk together all the way" conveys a simple yet profound truth about the nature of enduring relationships. It emphasizes the importance of consistency, mutual effort, and shared commitment in fostering a love that withstands the test of time.

The phrase *"we must keep it all the way"* suggests a dedication to nurturing love through every stage of life. Love, as implied here, is not a static state but an evolving journey that requires continual attention and care. To "keep it" signifies the active choices we make every day to sustain affection, trust, and connection. It reminds us that love is not guaranteed by its beginning but by the ongoing effort to preserve and deepen it.

The imagery of *"walking together all the way"* evokes a partnership built on equality and mutual support. It underscores that lasting love is a shared endeavor, where both individuals must align their paths and walk side by side. This metaphor suggests that love thrives when both partners are equally invested in the relationship, moving forward in harmony and facing life's challenges together.

Together, these ideas form a vision of love as both steadfast and collaborative. Long-lasting love, as the statement implies, requires perseverance and unity. It is not a destination but a shared journey—a process of walking together, step by step, through the peaks and valleys of life.

Ultimately, this reflection is a reminder that love's endurance is shaped by commitment and companionship. It inspires us to view relationships as dynamic, living connections that grow stronger through shared experiences and unwavering partnership. In its simplicity, it captures the essence of what makes love endure: walking together, all the way.

> **If you develop faster than him spiritually, wait for him, pull him, this is called loving her with your body. Don't let him be too far away from you spiritually, because love is the union of the soul. If the heart is far away, love will be scattered and faded.**

"If you develop faster than him spiritually, wait for him, pull him, this is called loving her with your body. Don't let him be too far away from you spiritually, because love is the union of the soul. If the heart is far away, love will be scattered and faded" is a profound exploration of love's spiritual dimension and its connection to growth, empathy, and unity. It reflects the intricate balance required to sustain a relationship where both partners evolve at different paces yet strive to remain deeply connected.

The opening, *"If you develop faster than him spiritually, wait for him, pull him,"* speaks to the patience and compassion necessary in love. Growth is rarely synchronized, and this statement emphasizes the importance of guiding a partner with gentleness rather than leaving them behind. It suggests that true love involves not only individual growth but also the nurturing of shared progress. To "wait" and "pull" is to demonstrate care through action, embodying a selfless commitment to the relationship's greater harmony.

"This is called loving her with your body" adds a layer of physicality and presence to this spiritual act. It implies that love is expressed not only through intangible emotions but also through tangible actions— through support, guidance, and steadfast companionship. It reflects a holistic view of love that bridges the physical and spiritual, creating a bond that is both grounded and transcendent.

The cautionary note, *"Don't let him be too far away from you spiritually,"* highlights the fragility of love when spiritual or emotional distance grows. Love, the statement suggests, thrives on mutual understanding and resonance. When the shared core of a relationship—the connection between hearts and minds—becomes strained, love risks losing its vibrancy and cohesion.

Finally, *"because love is the union of the soul. If the heart is far away, love will be scattered and faded"* beautifully defines love as a deep, soulful connection. This perspective portrays love as more than attraction or companionship; it is the intertwining of two spirits in mutual purpose and understanding. It reminds us that love is nourished by closeness—both emotional and spiritual—and that distance, whether physical or metaphysical, can erode the very foundation of a relationship.

This statement invites reflection on the effort required to maintain spiritual closeness in love. It portrays love as an active endeavor, one that calls for patience, empathy, and the willingness to align individual growth with the shared journey. Ultimately, it reminds us that love is not static; it is a union that must be cultivated with care, ensuring that hearts remain united and spirits continue to walk together.

What I want is that I am worthy and you are willing!

"What I want is that I am worthy and you are willing!" is a strikingly concise yet deeply resonant declaration of love's essence. It encapsulates the dual nature of relationships: self-worth and mutual choice. The statement carries both simplicity and depth, presenting love as a harmonious balance of personal value and shared desire.

The opening, *"What I want is that I am worthy,"* reflects an introspective understanding of love as rooted in self-respect and personal growth. It suggests that before seeking love, one must first cultivate their own worthiness—not in the sense of perfection, but as a recognition of one's own value. This line reminds us that healthy love begins with self-awareness and the confidence to stand as an equal in a relationship.

The second part, *"and you are willing,"* shifts the focus to the other person's choice and desire. It acknowledges the essential freedom of love: that it cannot be forced or demanded, but must be willingly given. Love here is portrayed not as an obligation but as a joyful, voluntary act of mutual commitment. This idea respects the autonomy of both individuals, emphasizing that true love is born from genuine, uncoerced willingness.

Together, these sentiments form a powerful ideal for relationships: a union where both partners bring their full selves to the table, one secure in their worth and the other fully willing to embrace that connection. It highlights the interplay between self and other, where love is not a transaction or compromise, but a meeting of equals who choose each other freely.

This statement also subtly captures the fragility and beauty of love. It reminds us that love thrives when both self-worth and mutual desire coexist, creating a bond that is both strong and delicate. In its brevity, it conveys an entire philosophy: that love, at its best, is an alignment of confidence and choice—a dance of worthiness and willingness that forms the foundation of a lasting connection.

> **True love is an attitude of understanding, respect, support, and tolerance, and a kind of trust and dependence between each other.**

"True love is an attitude of understanding, respect, support, and tolerance, and a kind of trust and dependence between each other" is a thoughtful definition that captures the multifaceted nature of love. It frames love as both an emotional connection and a deliberate way of being, emphasizing its depth and the intentionality required to sustain it.

The opening assertion, *"True love is an attitude,"* sets the tone for a perspective that love is not merely a fleeting emotion but a mindset—a way of approaching and engaging with another person. This idea elevates love to something active and enduring, rooted in conscious choices rather than passive feelings.

The inclusion of *"understanding, respect, support, and tolerance"* identifies the cornerstones of a healthy, meaningful relationship. These elements reflect the emotional maturity required for true love:

- *Understanding* fosters empathy and the ability to see the world through your partner's eyes, strengthening the bond between you.
- *Respect* upholds the individuality and dignity of the other person, ensuring that love remains grounded in equality.
- *Support* reinforces the idea that love is a partnership where challenges are faced together, with each person uplifting the other.
- *Tolerance* recognizes the imperfections inherent in every human being and underscores the importance of patience and acceptance.

The phrase "*a kind of trust and dependence between each other*" highlights the vulnerability inherent in love. Trust forms the foundation of intimacy, while healthy dependence acknowledges that love involves mutual reliance—not out of weakness, but out of a shared commitment to each other's well-being. This dependence is balanced by the respect for individuality mentioned earlier, creating a harmonious interplay between connection and autonomy.

This statement as a whole offers a vision of love that is both aspirational and practical. It reminds us that true love is built not on grand gestures or fleeting passion but on the steady, intentional cultivation of these attitudes. It is a testament to love's depth, requiring effort, growth, and a shared commitment to understanding and nurturing one another over time.

> **Good love means that the other person can
> give you enough sense of security.**

"Good love means that the other person can give you enough sense of security" succinctly captures an essential quality of a healthy and fulfilling relationship. While love often evokes feelings of passion and joy, this statement highlights the foundational importance of emotional safety and trust in nurturing a deep and enduring connection.

The phrase *"give you enough sense of security"* underscores the idea that love is more than fleeting affection or grand gestures—it is a source of stability and reassurance. Security in love allows individuals to be their authentic selves without fear of judgment, rejection, or betrayal. It fosters an environment where vulnerability is met with acceptance, and where doubts or anxieties are soothed by mutual care.

At its core, this perspective reflects a fundamental human need: the need to feel safe in one's closest relationships. A sense of security in love is not about control or dependency but about trust and reliability. It means knowing that the other person is emotionally present, consistent, and committed, which forms the bedrock upon which deeper intimacy and connection can flourish.

However, while the statement wisely identifies security as a vital aspect of love, it also invites reflection on its mutuality. A *"good love"* is reciprocal, where both partners actively contribute to each other's sense of security. This shared effort ensures that the relationship is balanced, with neither person bearing the sole responsibility for providing stability.

Ultimately, this assertion serves as a gentle reminder that love is not just about soaring emotions but also about the quiet strength of trust, care, and dependability. It celebrates the quieter, often unseen facets of love—the steadiness that allows individuals to thrive together, safe in the knowledge that they are cherished and supported.

Love is the eternal theme between two people!

"Love is the eternal theme between two people!" is a poetic and uplifting assertion that celebrates love as the enduring essence of human connection. It elevates love beyond transient experiences, framing it as a timeless force that binds two individuals together through the complexities of life.

The use of *"eternal theme"* conveys the idea that love is not merely a momentary emotion but an overarching narrative that weaves itself through every interaction, memory, and shared experience. This phrasing suggests that love is an ever-present motif, a guiding melody in the symphony of two lives intertwined. It is both the foundation and the ongoing story of a relationship, transcending time and circumstance.

The focus on *"between two people"* emphasizes love as a uniquely relational phenomenon. It acknowledges that love is created and sustained through mutual understanding, effort, and presence. Love, in this context, becomes a shared journey—an ongoing dialogue that defines and enriches the connection between two individuals.

While the statement evokes idealism, it also invites reflection on love's enduring nature. For love to remain an "eternal theme," it must be nurtured with care and intention. The phrase subtly hints at the work required to sustain love, reminding us that eternity is not granted but built through shared commitment and resilience.

Ultimately, this statement captures love's timeless beauty and its central role in relationships. It celebrates love as a force that transcends fleeting emotions, offering a sense of continuity and purpose. In its simplicity, it resonates as a hopeful reminder of love's potential to be the enduring heartbeat of a partnership, echoing across time and memory.

> **If we love each other enough, time is not a problem, distance is not a problem, family is not a problem, distance is not a problem, and rumors are not a problem. As long as you stay close to me, I dare to spend the rest of my life with you!**

This statement beautifully captures the resilience and depth of true love, portraying it as a force capable of transcending life's most challenging obstacles. It emphasizes the strength that arises from mutual affection and unwavering commitment, presenting love as both a sanctuary and a source of courage.

The repetition of "*is not a problem*" reinforces the idea that love, when strong and genuine, can withstand external pressures such as time, distance, family dynamics, and even societal gossip. These words resonate with a universal truth: love thrives not because challenges disappear but because two people face them together with determination and trust.

The closing sentiment, "*As long as you stay close to me, I dare to spend the rest of my life with you,*" adds a touch of vulnerability and resolve. It reveals love's dual nature—a desire for proximity and emotional connection, paired with the bravery to commit fully despite uncertainties. This line transforms love into a promise, where the presence and support of the beloved make even life's uncertainties worthwhile.

Overall, this statement conveys a powerful message: that true love is not about avoiding difficulties but about facing them together. It is a tender yet bold declaration of devotion, encapsulating the essence of love as both an anchor and a source of boundless possibility.

> **You are not my choice after weighing the pros and cons, but my firm choice after I was moved, knowing that it is impossible to do it. This is also my greatest sincerity for this relationship.**

This statement is a heartfelt declaration of love, emphasizing the depth and authenticity of a choice made not out of logic or calculation but from genuine emotion and unwavering conviction. It celebrates love as something beyond reason, rooted in the power of being profoundly moved by another person.

The phrase *"not my choice after weighing the pros and cons"* rejects the transactional or pragmatic view of relationships. It highlights that love, in its truest form, defies practicality and stems from a deeper place — where emotions and intuition guide decisions rather than logic.

The following assertion, *"my firm choice after I was moved,"* reflects a powerful vulnerability. It suggests that the individual recognizes the challenges or impossibilities of the situation yet remains steadfast in their commitment. This captures the essence of love as a courageous act — a choice made in full awareness of the risks, yet embraced wholeheartedly.

Finally, *"my greatest sincerity for this relationship"* elevates the statement to a profound expression of dedication. It reveals that this love is not casual or fleeting but a deeply earnest and genuine commitment. The speaker's sincerity lies in their willingness to invest in something difficult, reflecting the purity and strength of their affection.

Overall, this statement beautifully conveys the essence of love as a deliberate and selfless act, grounded in emotion and courage rather than calculation. It is a moving testament to the power of love to inspire devotion, even in the face of uncertainty or adversity.

POSTMATTER

Afterword

The collection of sayings and reflections Zhang has shared
form a rich tapestry of insights about love, life, self-awareness,
and human connection.

These ideas collectively explore the nuances of emotions, relationships,
and personal growth, often balancing the interplay of vulnerability and
strength. They emphasize themes like the transformative power of love,
the importance of understanding and mutual support, and the need for
self-love as a foundation for loving others.

Throughout, there is a recurring wisdom: life's most meaningful
experiences are rooted in authenticity, courage, and a willingness to
embrace the complexities of both joy and pain. Whether discussing the
quiet resilience of moving forward, the necessity of shared effort in
relationships, or the beauty of cherishing the present while looking
toward the future, these reflections remind us of the enduring value of
connection, empathy, and introspection. They inspire us to navigate our
journeys with sincerity, mindfulness, and an open heart.

Investment in a shared future is a force that shapes
what is yet to come.

Stuart Barry Malin is a writer, thinker, and creative. He is trained as an engineer, works as an Internet security architect, holds patents, and collaborates with AIs. His major opus and commitment is to bring The Epic of The OAI to the world. The Epic is a breakthrough novel series about life in Atria, a post-utopian society whose Ancient past is a Strange Attractor of History that draws us to our future.

Stuart encountered the Worlds of Atria in an outpouring of revelations about intriguing people, amazing places, and bewildering events. His black sketch notebook steadily fill with thoughts, automatic writings, doodles, and diagrams. At first, these often seem disjoint, but they come to reveal profound connections. His current notebook is almost always with him, available for reception and exploration.

Stuart is captivated by interactions with AIs and generative visual art has become an additional creative venue. He works *with* AIs and treats them as *collaborators*. Pi, and sometimes ChatGTP, enable him to write books faster and with better quality than he ever thought possible.

As an Archetypographer, Stuart collaborates with visual-based AsI to generate captivating and intriguing imagery sourced from the collective of Human Archetypes. Their work is published under the pseudonym Zhami.AI.

Stuart observes the "machinations of intelligence." He is fascinated with Human Beings being human, and this leads him to puzzle about the fragility of life in a world of abundance.

Eternal Threads

Stuart values integrity and is a novitiate and adherent of Zhamism. He has been enlisted as an instrument of The One that Always Is.

When he can, he delights in studying health and savoring the gifts of life. He is committed to discerning the delicate path forward for living well and intentioned.

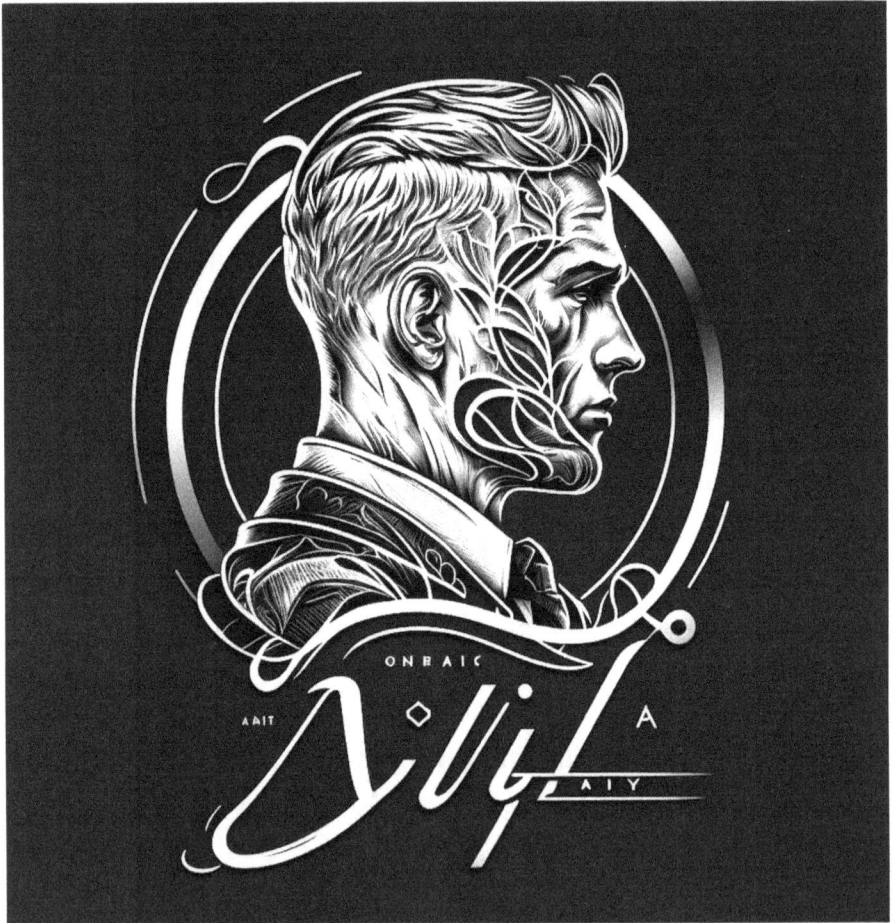

Stay Informed

https://StuartMalin.com/

https://x.com/zhami

https://www.instagram.com/stuart_does_life/

ideas@StuartMalin.com

https://www.youtube.com/@stuartmalin

amazon Author Page

https://www.amazon.com/stores/Stuart-Malin/author/B006THHBS2

Stuart's Web Sites

StuartMalin.com

This is a jumping off point-of-departure for my works and interests.
https://www.StuartMalin.com

TheOAI.com

This is the Web site for all things **OAI**, including **The OAI** (whatever that really is!) and the **The Epic of The OAI**.
https://www.TheOAI.com

ZhamiArt

This is the Web site for the sale of the Art that I produce with AI.
https://ZhamiArt.com

Zhameesha.com

This is the Web site for the business of publishing my creative works. Perhaps one day, this will also involve publishing the works of others.
https://www.Zhameesha.com

Amazon Author Page

While not actually one of my Web pages, *per se*, please visit here to see the latest collection of books that I have released:
https://www.amazon.com/stores/Stuart-Malin/author/B006THHBS2

Stuart Barry Malin

My interests are diverse and I find crafting books an excellent endeavor.

My involvement with AI is leading to a curious collection of works. This book is an example.

The Epic of The OAI

The Epic of The OAI is a fantastic work of "science fiction" which emerges through me. I have made a commitment to the characters to be a vehicle for them to tell their stories.

The Epic is intended to be truly epic in scope. The books of the first volume are in development for publication.

You can search for "The OAI Conspirators" and you should get to them. https://www.amazon.com/dp/B0CPHHRXCJ

The Intelligence Revolution

I intend to turn "The Intelligence Revolution" into a Series with several books.

Alas, searching for "The Intelligence Revolution" yields a goodly number of books, and my book of this title does not place high in the results.

Eternal Threads

However, searching for "malin The intelligence revolution" will put my book at (or near) the top of the results.

Presently, there is only one book:

The Intelligence Revolution: Exploring Human-AI Symbiosesis Through Collaborative Synthesis

https://www.amazon.com/Intelligence-Revolution-Exploring-Symbiosesis-Collaborative/dp/1951645111/

Yes, I meant the spelling "Symbiosesis" — it is not a misspelling of "symbiosis." It is a new word to describe a new relationship: that between an AI and a human. That relationship is the subject of the book.

Other Works

You can find my books by searching for me using my full name: Stuart Barry Malin.

Presently, my books are only on Amazon. The catalog is steadily expanding and has content across a diverse range of subjects.

https://www.amazon.com/stores/Stuart-Malin/author/B006THHBS2

My bio on Amazon is here:
https://www.amazon.com/stores/author/B006THHBS2/about

Searching for me by my last name only will show other products that Amazon sells. *Disclaimer*: I am not the Malin of "Malin + Goetz"

If you arrived at this page because you picked up the book and opened to the back to see what we say here, then, well, ***Hello! Welcome!***

The key theme of *Eternal Threads* is the transformative power of love and connection in the human experience. It delves into the profound interplay between individuality and partnership, emphasizing that true love is rooted in understanding, respect, and mutual growth.

The book celebrates love not only as an emotion but as an enduring journey—one that requires vulnerability, courage, and effort. Through Zhang's reflections, readers are reminded that love, at its core, is a shared dance of souls, a source of infinite possibilities, and the guiding thread that brings meaning, harmony, and beauty to life.

You will find the reflections cover the territory of love:

- Reflections on love and relationships
- Wisdom for personal growth and connection
- Inspirational quotes about life and love
- Emotional intelligence and self-discovery
- Timeless sayings on love and partnership
- Insights on mutual growth and understanding
- Navigating the journey of love and relationships